In the fall of 1997, I traveled all around the United States, shooting, mostly from hired helicopters, pictures of America's most sprawling manworks. Then I returned to Cape Cod and wrote this book about the experience. The trip and the printing were made possible by two grants from Chicago's Graham Foundation, and I am most grateful to its Board of Trustees and to its Executive Director, Richard Solomon, for their generosity and help.

MALCOLM WELLS

"Desert Disneyland"

The illustration on the preceding pages is my vision of Disneyland as it might look if all the roads and parking lots now surrounding it, as well as all the amusements, were put under deep layers of earth, allowing the desert to bloom again after all the years it's spent buried under those vast areas of lifeless asphalt and building materials. See p. 102.

These are my other books. As you can see, I've been at it for a long time. The asterisks indicate out-of-printedness, titles with no publisher named were self-published.

* SOLARIA, with Harry Thomason & Bob Homan.   •Edmund Scientific Co.

* ENERGY ESSAYS   •Edmund Scientific Co.

* HOW TO BUY SOLAR HEATING WITHOUT GETTING BURNT. •Rodale.
  with Irwin Spetgang.

UNDERGROUND DESIGNS

* NOTES FROM THE ENERGY UNDERGROUND •Van Nostrand

UNDERGROUND PLANS BOOK, with Sam Wells.

* GENTLE ARCHITECTURE   •McGraw-Hill

PASSIVE SOLAR ENERGY, with Bruce Anderson. •Brick House Publ.

* THE CHILDREN'S BOOK OF SOLAR ENERGY, with Tilly Spetgang.
  •Sterling Publishing Co.

BUILD A BETTER BIRDHOUSE   •Willow Creek Press

THE EARTH SHELTERED HOUSE   •Chelsea Green Publ. Co.

HOW TO BUILD AN UNDERGROUND HOUSE

THE SUCCESSFUL CONTRACTOR

BASEBALL TALK   •Willow Creek Press

PERSPECTIVE

INFRA STRUCTURES

MR. MANNERS

THE OLD TREE

SANDTIQUITY, with Kappy Wells & Connie Simo. •Willow Creek Press.

Write to me for a list of details and prices.

4.

Recovering America

I did all the drawings, watercolors,
and photographs except for those noted
on pages 60, 74-75, 85, 90, and 129.
Back cover photo by Andreas Moser.

— Malcolm Wells.

Printed in Singapore.

I.S.B.N.   0-9621878-8-7

First printing   October, 1999   2500
Second printing   February, 2000 10,000

My wife, Karen, and I own a
small gallery here on Cape
Cod. In it she produces and
sells her art, and I run a
one-man architectural
office. The building is
covered with a deep layer
of earth in which native
plants of all kinds are
thriving. Not surprisingly,

7.

we call the building Underground Art Gallery.

I make my living selling books on underground architecture, by designing earth-covered buildings, and by giving lectures and writing articles on this more gentle way to build.

Karen and her employees run the art gallery, but occasionally, when they're away, I deal with her customers. It was in that capacity that I greeted a visitor on a particularly hot day last summer.

"This air conditioning feels wonderful," she said.

"It's not air conditioning. Being underground keeps the building cool."

"What do you mean, 'underground'?"

She hadn't even noticed the vines and grasses that had made her duck outside the front door. I pointed to them and told her of the hundreds of tons of earth over our heads.

"Oh, my goodness! I never heard of such a thing."

So I gave her a brief run-down on underground architecture, and told her about the damage that conventional buildings do to land. She gave me

fish eyes in response. Uncomprehending.
It was obvious that she'd never looked
at the world around her, nor had she
ever heard of the environmental crisis.
Clearly, she thought she'd stumbled onto
a certified, dyed-in-the-wool nutcase.

She was one of the few people I'd
met during the preceding 25 years who
weren't charmed, even thrilled, to discover
the wonders of an earth-covered building and to think of its potential for
turning our land green again.

But I knew when I was licked. As
soon as I saw the curtain come down
across her mind I knew it would be use-
less to go on, so I thanked her for visit-
ing the Gallery and showed her to the
door.

God knows what she told the folks
at home that night.

———

We have a long way to go.

9.

In Boston, the life-giving edge of the sea has b

completely paved-over with buildings and docks.

In New Orleans, a bowl too big for cereal crushe

house c

...e life out of rich delta land in order to ...sional sporting events.

13.

And near Los Angeles, the flowering desert has

obliterated by a huge amusement park called Disneyland.

Far worse than the somewhat temporary damage done by herbicides - or hurricanes - the habitat destruction caused by the act of construction kills land for generations.

So here we are, in the middle of a great environmental tragedy, and we're seldom even aware of it! We've lived with above-ground buildings for so long it's almost impossible to see them for what they are.

We look at architecture the wrong way: sideways, so what we see is only a thin sliver of the reality all around us. A bit of landscaping, which is in reality only window dressing, can often make the most brutal land-killer, the most barren desert of asphalt, look relatively benign:

To see architecture fully you must tip it up, stand it on its edge!

When you do, you always see dead land on display. That's why I took all the aerial photos. How can the alternative to paving be anything but earth-cover? Land is either dead or alive. All we have to do is get over our prejudices against having gardens and forests over our heads and we'll be set to go.

But first, remember:

Underground architecture does not mean this:

Nor does it mean this:

It means simply this:

1.

BUILD A STRONG, WATERPROOF BUILDING. INSULATE IT. COVER IT WITH EARTH.

2.

3. AND PLANT IT WITH NATIVE PLANTS.

Consequently, all the interiors are bright and dry, and the views from all the windows are wide and green.

But getting back to my travel grant, I made the big U.S. trip and I must say I did it just in time. We've built over far more of America's best land than I'd ever imagined. From New Hampshire to California, from Seattle to Mobile, I saw thousands of square miles of what was once healthy land buried beneath roofs beyond counting; beneath parking lots for gazillions of cars; beneath eight-, ten-, twelve-, and sixteen-lane freeways; miles of toxic green lawns — even in the desert! — and lifeless rivers and harbors.

It was a shattering experience, seeing what we've done to all the miles of forests, the leagues of desert, the vast prairies: America, forgotten, under the malls and the ugliness.

Yes, I made the trip just in time. Another few hours, it seemed, and we'd have paved the whole damned continent.

To a degree, of course, I'd expected all that. What I hadn't expected were two

19.

other things, 1) the kindness of so many people in every part of the country, and 2) the incredible wealth and power – the raw muscle – of this nation! The distribution of that wealth and power is tragically skewed but the extent of it, of our resources, both human and natural, is truly staggering. It's Walt Whitman's America writ large.

I saw highway construction projects – big ones – some of which ran on for hundreds of miles. I saw huge buildings by the thousands. Vast industrial areas. Strip mines eating whole mountains. Forests – or rather former forests – denuded as far as the eye could see. Farms too big to comprehend. Thousands upon thousands of shiny new automobiles. Housing tracts

springing up everywhere. Busy airports with jumbo jets taking off one after another all day long. And of course all the new strip malls and shopping centers.

So don't tell me we don't have the resources, and the resourcefulness, to bring this land back to life. Hell, if we'd all just disappear for a while the natural world would do the job by itself.

I find it touching to see plants growing up through cracks in the concrete. Wonderful!

It brings tears of joy to my eyes when I see grass taking over an abandoned parking lot. What better sign of hope can there be than life's power to beat the asphalt odds? Here in the northeast where I live, freezing weather makes more cracks than Jay Leno,

and the abundant rainfall helps seeds to germinate in them. But even in the desert southwest I saw the same miracle occurring: nature trying, with silent eloquence, to show us the way things should be.

Of course along with America's great show of strength I saw the pollution too... all the ugliness and waste that a huge industrial economy — at least a huge 20th century industrial economy — seems bound to produce. Every time I saw it, which was, as you can imagine, almost constantly, I couldn't help but think how beautiful and clean this land will be when we do what nature intends for us to do. It's what I intend too. So we've got a powerful team going for the green. Me and nature.

My 25 years of experience with earth-cover construction proved to me long ago that the underground advantages are far greater than even their advocates sometimes

LANDSCAPE BY SHIRLEY DORKIN

realize. Not only does a living roof restore a dead site to life, it offers silence,

permanence, protection from the weather, and of course amazingly low heating and cooling bills. Life on the roof conserves rainwater too; downpours don't

25.

go roaring into gutters
and spouts, catch-
basins and storm
sewers. Rain doesn't
cause flash floods and
streambed erosion
where there are plants
to hold and use it.
Rather, it seeps into the
rooftop soil and drips
slowly into the surround-
ing earth. And when
it drips in the winter

it produces spectac-
ular icicles.
Underground buildings,
being permanent, are
not as likely to be de-
molished and replaced
every generation,
either. With them, you
change only the
occupancy and leave
the structures alone.
Undisturbed, the
rooftop plants
become ever more

luxuriant and
beautiful.
What a contrast
with my America
trip! I saw an
America that was
up for grabs:
tear down and
rebuild, tear
down and
rebuild, tear...

My travel experiences reminded me of the never-quite-perfected way of life we've rushed into. Much of my trip unfolded just as I'd planned it but I couldn't count on it. In addition to all _my_ wrong turns, reservations got mixed up, faxes didn't go through, computers were down, planes were late, roads always seemed to have detours, motel rooms weren't ready, light bulbs failed, drains got clogged, toilet paper ran out... I know, I know; I should have such problems. I don't mention them to suggest suffering. I had a great time in spite of the depressing theme of my trip. I mention the glitches only as a reminder that few manmade things work as

well as we expect them to. Take these silly gas station covers, for instance. One good blow or a tremor and bye-bye! Their only redeeming feature is their reminder, their hint, of the way future gas stations will look:

POROUS PAVING

Underground buildings, on the other hand, are almost storm-proof. I'm amazed that only a few have been built in "Tornado Alley!" They perform astonishingly well. The ones I've designed have never leaked. For 25 years they've just sat there, warm and dry, filled with sunlight, shielded from the elements that attack building materials.

It's possible that earthquakes can damage underground buildings. Earthquakes can damage whole continents. But I've yet to hear of such damage to earth-covered structures. The engineers I've talked with at underground conferences feel that these structures, being inherently strong, would fare better than their shaky above-ground counterparts.

The other forces that damage structures and paving — sunlight, acid rain, freezing — have little to get their teeth into when a protective living landscape stands guard over a building.

In this book, however, you're going to see an avalanche of bad news and just a trickle of good. Taken superficially, the avalanche spells serious trouble but the good news, you'll find, is all high-quality stuff. Potent. Rock solid. Inevitable. And very promising. The bad news is transient, ephemeral, perishable, precarious, evanescent, and, having consulted my thesaurus, temporary and unsupportable. (Or unsustainable, if you'd care to use today's catchword.) Life, in other words, is sure to prevail in the long run.

Once we get that message, watch out! We're in for a happy time. Talk about a green revolution! Imagine what it will be like when our world no longer looks like this:

My only regret is that I won't be able to catch the entire show. At 73 I won't have time. But that's just being greedy. The show has already quietly started, and I can see the rest of it in my head.

In the seventies everyone else who talked about earth shelter was talking about saving energy for himself by using the earth to shield his house from the more

extreme temperatures of summer and winter. Particularly winter.

As the years passed and the other advantages of earth shelter became apparent it was clear that we had in our hands a way to do a lot more than save energy. We could put back all the lovely forests and prairies we removed during the second half of the 20th century. How? Like this: the same way we removed them: one by one, as the opportunities came along.

Everyone who's lived or worked in an underground building has become a convert to the idea. In the silent world of the earth, looking out over a valley or a park or a distant mountain range, it's hard to understand why we haven't always built this way.

Think of all the possibilities!

On this earth there are perhaps millions of square miles of manworks. Or peopleworks if you wish. I have no idea what that area is but there's no question that it's more than we can imagine! Think of all the trees that will never exist in the forest that was replaced by this Massachusetts truck terminal. What a perfect candidate for a deep covering of earth on a rugged concrete roof!

Now, you may very well be wondering why, if this is such a burning issue, it's not in all the newspapers and on all the talk shows.

One answer, of course, is that the people who produce the news and the talk are not exactly what you'd call earth-attuned. Circulation - and ratings - usually drive their decisions. Can you picture a T.V. producer looking at her studio as she approaches it in the morning, thinking, "This is killing a forest and all of its inhabitants"? No. Even though a T.V. studio is just as good a candidate for a roof of trees and wildflowers as is the terminal on the left. And most in need of such a cover is the deadly surface that does nothing but provide parking for automobiles.

How in the world did we ever let ourselves get into this situation?

Across the Charles River from Boston, over in Cambridge, America's best-known engineering school, M.I.T, spreads into the city from this temple-like core.

M.I.T. offers many environmental courses but don't be fooled; love of nature is not their central motive. Their goal is to let us go on living pretty much the way we do now without paying too high a price in terms of pollution and shortages. Like most of us, M.I.T. isn't quite with it yet.

WGBH, Boston's public television station, is one of the best in the country, so while I was shooting Boston from the air I made sure to get a picture of it.

On the next page you'll see my version of it as an earth-covered building. You might at first think that WGBH looks natural enough as is, considering all the trees, but they're little more than window dressing; that site is almost dead, no more than 5% alive. It broadcasts death.

39.

As you can see, this photo was taken in the year 2003, just before Western Avenue was put underground.

What would our world be like if we always considered the well-being of land first? It would certainly be a lot greener, cleaner, and quieter, but would it bring about the end of all the other crises that fill the headlines? Hardly. It might not affect them at all, although I can't believe it, not when all the dead surfaces around us so eloquently express the despair in so many lives.

The rules of life never change:

1. People can't draw energy directly from sunlight.

2. Plants can.

3. Plants can't live underground.

4. We can.

It's as simple as that. Underground with windows gives us the best of both worlds. Whether the great towers of center city will ever have gardens on their roofs doesn't matter very much. It's all those far-flung miles around downtown that must be recalled to life.

42.

The towers of downtown may come to have less of an environmental impact when two things unrelated to underground construction come into play. One is the emerging work-at-home promise of the computer. The other is the electric car.

When most office work, and even factory work, is done from home the current boom in industrial and commercial buildings is sure to fade, and more of our resources can be put toward restoring life to the land. And when vehicles are powered by non-polluting engines, underground highways will smell a lot better. (Without such engines things could get a tad smoky under the new forests and grasslands of America.)

So the prospect hence, as Thoreau said, is infinite. Who knows what inventor, hard at work right now in her garage workshop, will bestow on us an idea so appropriate, so timely, that the whole restoration movement will race ahead of our best current schedules for it?

But today everyone seems to assume that the natural

environment is bound to get worse. .
We're not shocked when people ask, "Is it
still nice where you live?" We seem to
have accepted as inevitable the idea
that despite occasional impressive up-
scale successes in restoring old
neighborhoods or replanting woodlands
the trend will be forever downward.

It had taken me years to realize that the
big industrial buildings I was designing
were actually destroying land. America's
land. All I saw were the big fees and the
glory. I also did offices, labs, churches,
a world's fair building, libraries, and
even — I blush to admit it — an environmental center, all of them above ground!
And then, even after I'd discovered that
underground design offered the best
possible theme for architecture, it still
took me years to see that this new/
old way onto which I'd stumbled was
perhaps the _only_ right way to build.

A lot of architects would smile at such
arrogance. I wouldn't blame them.
From where they sit, this little pipsqueak

environmental movement will go no-
where. But I've done the killer buildings
and I've done the healer-buildings, and
they can speak for themselves.

How I wish I could wave a wand and
make early designs of mine like these
disappear!

Anyway,
with the travel
grant safely in
the bank and my pockets stuffed with trav-
elers checks I left for my first stop: New
Hampshire.

I wanted some shots of northern forests
and I wanted to see what had been done
to that lovely state in the years since I'd
last been there.

New Hampshire!
The nice parts are gorgeous. The developed
parts? Well, I think this is where it's best
to say "don't ask."

It rained the whole day I was up there.
Sometimes I couldn't see 50 feet ahead
of the car. When it let up a bit I could see

torn scraps of cloud racing across the dark mountains. Beautiful. But it poured every time I got out of the car. I had to shoot quickly or get soaked. (shoot quickly _and_ get soaked was more like it.) That was OK. Rain seemed appropriate to those mossy forests and rushing streams.

i couldn't get
enough of them.

I <u>could</u> get enough of the
man-made destruction. After

49.

I'd shot one giant mall in the downpour home began to sound better and better. I couldn't take the contrast between what was so obviously so right for New Hampshire and what was obviously so wrong.

I decided not to stay overnight, and drove all the way home, back to Cape Cod, where Karen had had time to pick enough blueberries for a pie after I called her, and I walked into a house filled with a heavenly aroma. It made that dead sheet of wet asphalt at the New Hampshire mall seem light years and not just hours away.

A few days later, I arranged to shoot the Cape Cod Mall from a helicopter. Door off. The Mall abuts the Hyannis airport so I was taking pictures a minute or two after we'd lifted off. Click. Click. Click.

I just kept shooting till we'd been around the buildings twice.

Seeing them through the viewfinder hid some of the impact that eyeballing alone would have caught; it wasn't till I'd gotten the pictures

back that I could appreciate the true extent to which nature had been wiped out. An entire forest was gone!

Cape Cod, being a sandy spit left behind by a glacier, does not have what you'd call rich soil, especially since it's been cut over, farmed, and eroded for close to 400 years, but its forest is still fairly rich and diverse as it struggles to put back some of what was removed.

At the Mall everything had been removed. Trees, shrubs, topsoil, streams, birds, insects, animals - gone. Gone for the purpose of parking cars and sheltering

People! The windowless buildings almost cry out for earth cover. But no; hour after hour, day after day, even when the Mall is closed, those lifeless materials block the soil from rescue by the forest that rightfully belongs there.

My next destination, if I could find it, was an abandoned shopping center in northern New Jersey not far from the George Washington Bridge. A year earlier, I'd been told that wild-flowers were taking over the parking lot there. Just what I wanted!

I rented a car and plunged directly into 70-mile-an-hour traffic on the Garden State (hah!) parkway, realizing too late that my eyesight and my reaction time weren't at all what they used to be.

"Jesus, Mac," I said, knuckles white, "you're too old for this shit."

I was a positive hazard to other drivers as I raced along in the curb lane looking for the Route 4 exit. Miles later, when I was sure I'd missed the turn, I got off into a maze of one way - the wrong way - streets and could find no one to give me directions. I had to wing it and wish for the best. Then suddenly there it was? Alexander's!

To my eyes it couldn't have looked nicer.
Grass everywhere. And trees! New Jersey
trying to turn into New Jersey again.
Click. Click. Click.

entrance

parking

EXIT ↑

EXIT

WELLS
'97

And - my goodness! - what's this? Why it's an underground shopping center! And already it's sprouting more wildflowers than that N.J. parking lot. Looks promising. About 2004 A.D.?

Also promising is this building I did in the mid-sixties for Construction Fasteners near Reading, Pennsylvania. Partly bermed, partly underground, its once-barren site has by now turned into a forest, with water-conserving sunken gardens and wildlife ponds.

(I often manage to catch the blackest of blacks when I take pictures on bright days but perhaps you'll overlook that and concentrate on the landscaping.)

An island of vegetation, shelter, and water like this attracts unbelievable numbers of wild creatures. Some are migratory, others stick around. Construction Fasteners is surrounded by an 8-lane freeway, a big shopping center, and several ordinary office/factory buildings, each with its toxic green lawn, its dot-dot-dot landscaping, and its conventionally-drained roofs and parking lots that repel and waste all the rain that falls on them rather than using it on the parched sites. As a consequence, city water has to be brought in from miles away to do the watering.

Am I missing something or are we going about things in a crazy way?

Next, our fearless aerial photographer was ready for the big shoot, and on the following morning, across the Potomac at Washington National Airport, the helicopter was waiting. It wasn't a little mosquito like the one I'd hired on Cape Cod. This was a plush, six-seat animal, and its big side door was wide open.

I knew we wouldn't be shot down but I couldn't help wondering, if we were, if the obituary would mention the advantages of underground architecture.

Once in the air, I could see the famous 5-sided

structure. I had known, generally, what it would look like but I was utterly unprepared for its size or for the size of the parking lots serving it.

From the ground, the Pentagon looks relatively parklike and green, but from above....
whew! I had to keep asking the pilot

to back away so I could get more of that
asphalt into my viewfinder. Cars, cars,
cars; more than even Rainman could count.
Click click click. Look at all that military
precision, all that military-based land
destruction.

Instead of thinking only of that, though, I
felt other thoughts intruding: What must it
be like for a woman to walk alone on a
dark winter evening to the most remote cor-
ner of one of those mega-lots to find her car?
The top brass don't have far to walk. Look→
They have covered (not earth-covered) parking
right by the front door. Rank has its privi-
leges.

And what of those hugely wasteful activities inside the Pentagon's walls, inside those five-sided walls, inside those five-floored, five-ringed spaces? I was one of the millions of us paying for it all, and I wasn't too happy about it, even if I could turn the place into a five-sided underground master-piece.

Hmm.... well why not? The strong, fort-like shape is perfectly suited to the solid look of an earth structure. And the parking could be on five levels only a short walk from the offices.   Hmm... let's give it a try...
...several tries, in fact.   Take a look.→

When the Great Forest of Virginia comes
surging back across the dying land, deep
soil will cover not only this alternative

64.

Pentagon but also the parking levels and the highways surrounding it. Quite a change from the toxic lawns and the asphalt seen there now.

or why
not raise
it on
huge
pylons
and
let the
earthen
base
express
its
earthiness
?

Notice
the
forest
even
on the
office
roof.

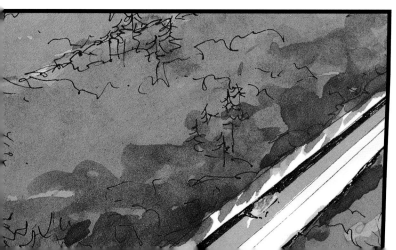

The Raven Rocksers, as I sometimes call them, are a group of about a dozen Ohioans who scraped and borrowed and earned enough money to save several hundred acres of spectacularly scenic forest and ravine land before it could be sold to the strip miners.

Rich and Mary Sidwell are just completing their solar underground house there, and I'm itching to show it to you, but it was in those last stages of construction, just before the earth went onto the roof, when the promise was so great and the reality so raw. I could hardly bear to shoot it. Here's a drawing instead.

OK. Maybe I'll show you a photo, too, just a little one, a glimpse. And maybe, if the Sidwells send me a good snapshot before I get this book printed, I'll show  you even more. The best picture in the world, however, won't begin to describe the Sidwells' sunny interiors with their sweeping views in three directions over the rolling hills and the forests of what is called "The Switzerland of Ohio." You won't see all the careful cabinetry, either. The Raven Rocksers don't hire people to do their construction work. They do it all themselves.

All?

All.

A few hundred feet away, out of sight beyond the trees, another solar earth shelter, a big one, is under construction by three other "Rocksers", Chris Joyner, Don **Hart**ley, and Warren Stet**zel**, who go by the

contraction **J. Hartzelbuck**, the "buck" part
belonging to Tim Starbuck, one of the four
who died a couple of years ago but who
continues to inspire them.

The big house, called Locust Hill, will not only
be a residence, it will act, as well, as a
demonstration of all the advantages of
building into the earth. In fact, in spite of its

location far
out in the
boonies on
a twisting
forest road,
it has already
attracted
visitors from
all over the
country.
They get an
eyeful there.
Even though
it's not
complete,
Locust Hill
is being so
well built,
and its
owners are
so well
informed

about everything
from wind power
and earth cover
to organic farming
and solar energy
that visitors come
away fired with
the land-care
idea.

If Construction
Fasteners in
Reading is a joy
to me in its adorn-
ment of my designs
the Raven Rocks
projects equally
please me with
the care and love

so apparent in the work. At Raven Rocks the
process is as important, and for them, as much
fun, as the product:

The main floor is on a couple of levels but basic-
ally the building is arranged as shown in the
cross section I am about to draw...

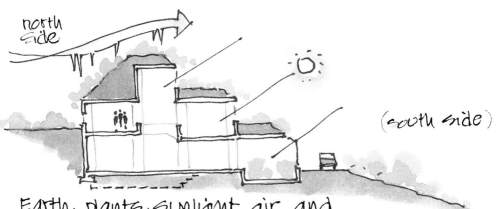

north
side

(south side)

Earth, plants, sunlight, air, and
a building that will last for hundreds of years.
The occupancy may change and the occupants,
certainly will but the hope is for the
flowering earth to live on, undisturbed.

south side

In this drawing of the north side you can see the long narrow band of windows that is shown on the north side of the cross section.

THE NORTHSIDE GARDEN AT LOCUST HILL
MALCOLM WELLS, ARCHITECT 8/89

Rich

Mary

The Gridwells did
send photos!
This was the day
the earth went
onto the roof.

74.

Mary and Rich
Sidwell, and
part of Mary's
vegetable
garden.

Next stop: Chicago, and another roaring highway; different from the others because I traveled it on foot this time, edging along a narrow sidewalk as the day was fading, kicking my way through beer cans and trash on my way to the restaurant the motel woman had said was only a block away. Hers was a mental block, apparently, for I had to walk 20 minutes to reach the place. We forget, when we drive, how great some distances are.

Walking quickly along the highway, aware of every sound which might be that of someone behind me on that lonely but roaring stretch

of Chicago's south side, I wondered if, when my dream of prairie-covered structures comes true, some future Malcolm, walking —along that flower-bordered underway, would feel any less threatened than I did.

The motel clerk who'd so badly estimated the

walking distance was the same one who'd
given me the wrong key – actually a magnet-
ically coded card – the key to an already-
occupied room. "Oops, sorry sir," I'd said,
backing out in a hurry as the man in the
nearest bed turned toward me in surprise.
When I returned the key I didn't expect an
apology and I didn't get one. That should
have told me that the woman's restaurant-
directions would be about as dependable as
her key selection. Courteous helicopter
people seemed far away.

Now, before the story of my imagined assail-
ants begins to make me sound like a white
racist I should explain that when I pictured
being mugged I pictured white men. I'd been
too well treated on my trip by black and
brown people to imagine any harm coming
from them. Naive, I know, but the kindest
and most helpful people throughout my trip
– kinder perhaps even than the general
aviation people – were the African-Americans
I'd asked for help in so many places. Sometimes I didn't even have to ask. Maybe they,
having been neglected when they needed help,
knew a lost look well enough to recognize
it in me and to offer assistance unasked.

Some people, knowing of my earth-cover convictions, like to kid me about putting airports underground, for they know that I favor that idea, too. They joke about the sizes and shapes of the slots into which the planes would land...

... or about underground airplanes!

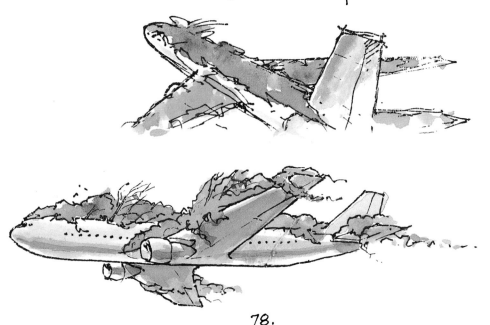

They find them easier to talk about than the real issues such as the appalling amount of land, often wetlands near rivers or bays, that airport buildings and runways cover.

The runways, of course, must be on top of the ground, as shown in this 1971 drawing of an underground airport, but everything else — hundreds

of thousands of square feet at every airport — is a prime candidate for under-the-gardens design.

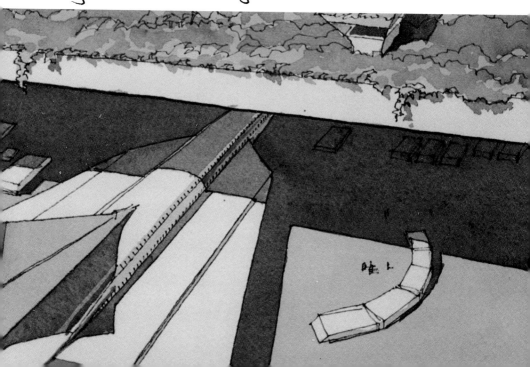

Great Salt Lake was another nice surprise.
It looked like an ocean with mountains
rising out of it! A Japanese landscape.
Beautiful. It wasn't hard to see why the
Mormons had settled there after their long
struggle to cross the Rockies.

Like many western cities, Salt Lake City has wide streets. I'm told that the width was established by the need for horses and wagons to turn around. OK. But why are all the <u>modern</u> residential streets so wide? Asphaltitis, that's what it is.

oops! ↗

SLC, as the city is often called, has many parklike places, some alive with flowers. It also has miles of the run-down gray industrial burbs that seem to coalesce around cities. Undergrounding all of them is going to keep us busy for years.

82.

Near the Mormon temple in the center of town giant planter-bowls as big as rooms overflow with flowers and shrubs, proving to all who pass that plants can indeed fare well when lifted above their mother. The bowls offer us another nudge toward successful earth cover.

On to Seattle and the worst driving mix-up of the trip. At Seatac Airport I successfully arranged by phone for a helicopter flight the next day, successfully rented a car, successfully made my way out of the airport, and then spent well over an hour trying to find the motel that was, in fact, only about a mile away! Finally, however, my elusive destination reached out and got me, and there my bladder could smile again. There, I could wash a week's undies and take a nap.

Now, you may very well get from all this the idea that I am not too bright, not someone to be trusted in any way, either for following travel directions or for spreading the good news about underground architecture. But that's not the case. None of my buildings have leaked — ever — and they've all been sunny, dry, silent, and a snap to heat, cool, and maintain.

Even my first underground building (right) which had no insulation, I blush to admit, has a thermal performance, both summer and winter, that outdoes comparable aboveground buildings in that regard.

84.

Basmajian

In the center of Seattle there's a beautiful park, a shady place full of levels and walls with plants spilling over the edges. On another trip, I'd happened to walk there, happy that I'd found such a perfect spot in the middle of the city. After blocks and blocks of lifeless concrete and steel, marble and glass, it was truly a relief.

I could hear the sound of traffic there in that little wooded area, and, standing on tiptoe to look over one of the walls, I saw a big freeway running under me!

Hooray! Way to go, Seattle!

Now, in the helicopter, I was looking down on that same scene, my earth-cover fires re-kindled by what I saw. Here was America, A.D. 2015, a bit early for its appointment with destiny.

But I forgot to take a picture! All I can offer is this 60 mph, through-the-windshield shot. Thank goodness for autofocus cameras!

We were helicoptering northward to shoot the world's largest building, Boeing's assembly plant at Everett, several miles from the city, the place where the 747s are put together.

By a strange coincidence (that he thinks was no coincidence) I'd gotten to know Malcolm Stamper, "Mr. 747" as he was called when he produced the first of those giant airliners. A few years ago, having no idea that he existed, I'd sent a children's-book proposal to a Seattle publishing company called Storytellers Ink. An enthusiastic response came from Mr. Stamper, and our friendship began. My children's book is still on hold but in the intervening years I've illustrated other books for Mal. He and I have discovered that our first names are quite similar, that we both went to Georgia Tech, and both went on to great success, he to head the world's largest aircraft manufacturing company, I to head an unknown 6-person, above-ground architectural office. There, I was destined to do a lot of conventional factories

and parking lots before a less destructive
way of building ever occurred to me.

When Mal retired from Boeing he wanted to do
something for kids.   Books — reading —
seemed to be the most effective choice.
somehow, he's been able, through grants, and
corporate sponsorships, and , I suspect, a
great deal of his own money, to publish dozens

of delightful books for children, and to make
them available at very little cost, to school
systems all around America, the idea being
to encourage reading and, through reading,
to instill in our next generation the ideas of
88.

kindness to others, to animals, and to the natural world. The kids take the books home with them, to keep. Sometimes those storytellers books are the only ones the kids have ever owned.

I'd fallen into an inspiring friendship when I connected with Mal and his company. Now here I was, flying through a local rain shower, almost too exhilarated by the flight to notice the raindrops, then emerging into clearer air to see ahead the plant that he'd built.

At first it didn't look very big. About the size of your average shopping mall. Then I noticed the cars.

That's when the scale of the structure hit me. That was one BIG building down there! Mal never brags about having built that megastructure. And he knows that my mission is not to criticize people responsible for such things. I did my own share of above-grounders. More than my share, I'd say.

Big buildings and their big products, by their

very size, are further proof that we have the know-how to do vast projects. And, combining that capacity with our emerging sense of how the world works, I see the stage set for an eye-popping turn-around.

The Everett plant has its own airport, and
Chris, my pilot, was careful to ask permission
for every move we made in proximity to it.

I could hardly wait to get home and do my
version of the way that mighty structure
would look sheltered by the new forest of
the northwest. Returned to life.

My first impression is on the next page.

Then off we flew, back to Seattle, as I continued to shoot pictures of what, for millenia, had been a great forest. As you can see, there was no shortage of subjects. Some of the paved areas down near the docks were astounding. It was land-contempt at its most flagrant: the Pacific forest, stripped away to provide storage for... automobiles!

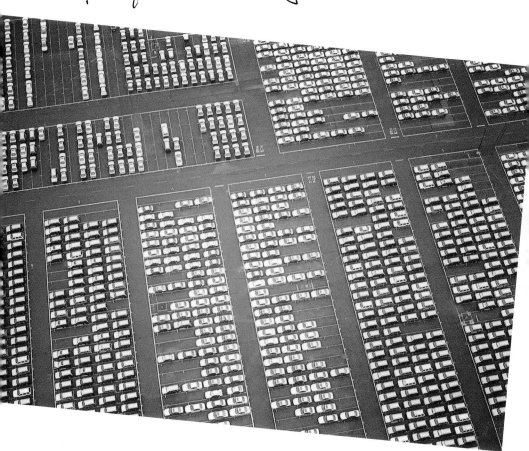

Talk about morals and values! Hah.
These pictures say it all.

L.A.X. at 11:15. Helicopter due at 12:30. Piece of cake. All I had to do was take a shuttle from Terminal 1 to Terminal 4, and go up to the heliport. I got there early, found the big HELIPORT sign, and found the door was locked!

Knock knock.
Nothing.
BANG BANG BANG!

The big airport went about its business with an unending roar.

Run back down-stairs. Public telephone. Airport manager's office. 11:35. "We'll send someone over right away with a key."

Run back up-stairs. 11:50.
12:00.
12:15.
Pace pace pace.
BANG BANG BANG!
("I'm getting too old for this!")

12:28. The door opened! But it wasn't the

airport's man. It was my pilot, Andreas Moser, right on time. He'd flown up from John Wayne Airport in Costa Mesa and, finding no one on the pad, had come down into the parking garage and opened the door. Ah, those general aviation people! I love 'em.

Maybe that lift-off wasn't an exciting ride!

Whew!... straight up off the roof, up by the control tower, with L.A.'s (above-ground) airport spread out below us. Parked in the sky as we awaited permission to cross those busy runways, we watched the big jets land and take off directly below us.

Click. Click. Click. Then it was off to the southeast, through L.A.'s famous curtain of airborne wastes, over ... well, let the pictures tell you what we were over.

Andreas, of course, knew exactly where we were at every moment; I saw only a carpet of sameness. Mile by mile, he pointed out landmarks in the murk. Our destination was Disneyland. I'd heard that its parking lot was world class in size (a feature of that fantasy kingdom not featured in the ads) so I expected to be impressed. The whole L.A. region is so heavily built-over I knew that the Disney asphalt would have to be vast to shock me — and it was! The famous amusement park was absolutely dwarfed — dare I say seven-dwarfed? — by its own dead zone. It was my first-ever look at a Disney theme park and I was appalled by it. There was no way I could get it all into a single photograph. I

dream of what the fabled Disney talent
will do when America learns to stop paving
land. That's when all the parking lots,

102.

roads, amusements, and hotels will be
covered with desert soil, allowing it to heal
its wounds and flower again.

103.

Then back we flew toward an L.A. that was out of sight somewhere, miles to the north-west. I saw another freeway ahead... no, it's a... what is it? It looks like a big concrete river of green slime. Is this another planet? Is there anyone alive today who remembers how that river once looked?

Twisting across that lovely desert, changing its course at will; free, it probably had giant cottonwoods growing wherever there were springs. Desert flowers, lions, eagles,

scorpions, silence, boulders and silvery drift-
wood, all of them under crystal-clear skies,
the now unseen mountains looking close
enough to touch.

The Great Artist I don't even believe in has a
way of arranging every natural scene with
utter perfection, effortlessly. But such scenes
are ever harder to find under all the paving.

The next day: Las Vegas!

Has anyone not seen pictures of the Strip?
Well, forget them. They no more represent
the real thing than this does. (This was taken
a few blocks away from the strip.) The Strip
is ten times bigger and brighter than you'd
imagine. Pictures can't begin to express the
overpowering hugeness and gaud of the
clustered casinos. Towering Mannekins,
— automated, of course — unbelievable roller
coasters, thousand-room hotels, and some
of the widest streets ever. Forget turning
wagons around in them. These were sized

to turn the Q.E.II!

Las Vegas is Atlantic City gone berserk, Atlantic city on a cosmic scale. And not a green plant to be seen. Wedding chapels next to topless bars and pawn shops. Then more huge hotels. Slot machines everywhere - in the motel, the airport, the supermarket. It was all too much, too big, too glittery for me to grasp.

Where do they get all the materials, the water, the energy? This is the desert. How do they handle all the sewage? Who pays for all this? The money involved must be astronomical. Sleaze taken to the tenth power.

107.

But the strip wasn't my first surprise. First was the heat. It was the first time I'd ever heard a cabin attendant ask those passengers staying aboard to lower their window shades against the sun. We'd come from very warm L.A. to blast furnace heat in 50 minutes. Wham! And then ... wait a minute: after a while it wasn't so bad. 105° but the humidity was low, not as low as it once was, now that pools — and green lawns! — dot the desert, but it was still dry enough to reduce the level of discomfort considerably.

My second surprise was the ring of mountains all around. Crackling crisp, sharp-

edged mountains in the bright sunlight. But they're not as close as they look. You must drive for miles to get to them, and it's worth it. They and the high-desert landscape that leads to them offer a glimpse of the Vegas that was, the Vegas that now sleeps its long sleep under the boulevards and the casinos.

Hoping for relief, I looked up the address of the Las Vegas Museum of Natural History, and, surprisingly, I found the place unaided. Surrounded by asphalt, it sits on a virtually treeless lot. It was late on a Saturday afternoon when I was there. The building was closed but I could imagine the busloads of school kids that would start to arrive on Monday. They'd be given the latest word on the state of nature. The official message

was no doubt green – like that water-hogging lawn across the street – but the site's visual message said something else.

Which one would the kids remember?

In sharp contrast to the natural history
museum there's a place called Demonstration
Gardens where desert flora are displayed
in simple, residential-scale settings created

to persuade homeowners to use less water and more native plants. As far as I could see, however, few Las Vegans have gotten the message. Where I didn't see toxic green lawns and east-coast trees I saw raked pebbles. Anything but – ugh! – what belonged there.

It wasn't till I visited Dave and Deanne Stoll that the Demonstration Gardens' impact was apparent. We'd exchanged letters for years but until then had never met.

The Stolls are creating a beautiful and appropriate landscape which uses only a small amount of water. Care to meet them?

Deanne is a ceram-ic artist. Dave is a carpenter. And what a carpenter! He's one of the brightest I've met and I don't say that just because he knows how to run one of those computer things. An avid reader and a gifted writer as well, he wrote in a recent letter something I'd like to quote for you:

"If humankind ever wakes up and realizes that we not only can but need to live in harmony with nature this will be the last place saved. Lots of people wince at the thought of a bulldozer taking down a forest but no one gives the slightest thought to blading off the desert. It's actually alive with plants and animals but most people think it's ugly and life-less. In an advertisement for tract homes here the caption was, 'Fill in The Blank'."

Dave and Deanne took me to see the new county building — click, click, click — about which Dave had written,

"The facade is brownish-red stone. All that thermal mass guarantees that the build-ing's air conditioning will be struggling 24 hours a day. The parking lot is several

acres of hot asphalt, some of it at least 1/4 mile from the building. The few (non-native) trees are placed in spots that make them worthless for shade. The alleged 'desert landscape' is mostly colored gravel spread over plastic, with sparse and inappropriate shrubs that get replaced on a regular

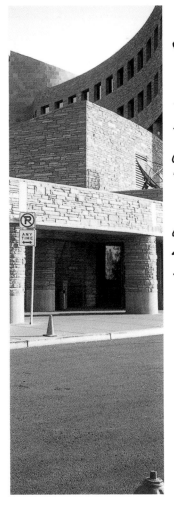

basis as they die. They are watered by impulse-type sprinklers, not by drip-irrigation. When the sprinklers are on, usually in the afternoon when the hot wind blows, people get their cars splattered as they drive on the nearby streets. My only pleasant thought about this building is that the designer knew what he was doing when he added the yardarm at the top. Obviously, the amphitheatre there would make a great place from which to view public hangings, one of which might involve those responsible for fleecing the taxpayers to finance this eyesore. Cost overruns were rampant, at least doubling the original $80 million estimate"

One book at that place and I agreed. Click, click, click.

—

Then it was off to New Orleans to look for the big dome.

Hours later, as I emerged from the tangle of downtown freeways, I saw the biggest nuclear reactor I'd ever seen. Or was it... could it be... the Superdome? It was! I parked the car and just stood there, bowled over by the menacing aura of that gigantic windowless tub. It is immense. I could hardly believe that

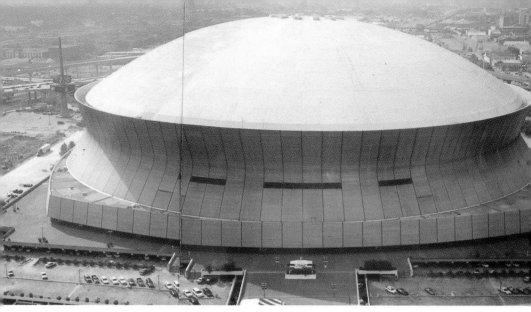

happy crowds, bright colors, and noise could at times bring such a place to life.

Obviously, aliens had landed there in River City, and they seemed to enjoy killing rich land as much as we do. What in the world, I wondered, would we think of such things 25 years from now.

My wondering got me thinking of a way to house huge sporting events, as well as all the cars involved, under a blanket of Louisiana forest land, and out came this squared circle punctuated by tall office towers at the corners. The towers need more thought but you get the idea.

↪

My friend, Terry Plauché, a Mobile landscape architect, promised to show me a tropical forest so I drove across the bottom of Mississippi, seeing mostly pines and bayous except where my fellow humans had gotten a foothold:

Biloxi

In places, it was New Jersey all over again, complete with strip malls, honky-tonk, fast foods, banners, and twinkles, all underlain, of course, with dead soil. Just like home ... anywhere.

But Terry took me away from all that. What a nice guy: he closed his office and took me to a natural area so dark and beautiful I

knew I'd be disappointed when the films were developed. It wasn't disappointing in person, however. What silent relief, what rightness the land put forth!

Mobile, Alabama

Home by way of Orlando. For a moment I
was tempted to get off the plane, rent one last
car, and shoot Disney World, but I thought
you'd need as much of a break from all that
as I did, so I stayed on the plane, shot a bit
of green Florida and a bit
of brown Florida before
buying a glass of beer and
taking a nap. I didn't
wake up until we were
letting down into the new
airport at Providence
from which I'd take a bus
home to Cape Cod.

The airport is called Green even though its color is gray. It's just one more missed opportunity for a startling new kind of airport building. But someday, one way or another,

Green Airport will be truly green.

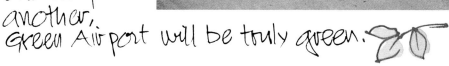

Please watch your step; there are 18 rolls of exposed film in that bag!

With my travel grant wearing thin I could count on shooting only one or two more cities. Nearby Boston was the next logical one, and perhaps a fitting last stop.
Karen agreed to close the Gallery and go along. It was, as I'd predicted, a delightful heli-

coptering exper-ience, delightful in all but the reality of what we saw down below. But even that's not true. There was so much _promise_ in being present near the end of America's paving era that the destruction on the ground could almost be read as a harbinger of all the good to come.
Karen (did I remember to tell you she's my wife?) and pilot Michael Peavey sat up front. I was in back, leaning out the window in the hurricane down-rush of the rotor blades, snapping pictures of our home city.
126.

Only in one place did we see Boston's ancient, appropriate, and necessary ground cover:

All the rest was just like this.

Boston

Even the water's edge
is gone, all paved over
with docks and roads
and buildings as if it
had no value at all!
Thank goodness we're
finally starting to
wake up.

128.

Paved
barrier
beach
at Cape
Cod.

Now, are
you ready?
Here's the
test
question:

Which is worse, to build on dry-
or on wetlands? Why, wetlands, of
course. They're the earth's most
productive breeding areas for plants
and animals.

Well then why has Boston, and virtually
every other city, covered the edge of
the sea with lifeless buildings and docks?

Boston harbor, ca. 1600

Ignorance, self-centeredness, short-sighted-ness... But not cruelty. We destroyed it in total innocence.

Mary McConnell Taylor

A group in rural Ontario, concerned about the minimum-security facility to be built near their town, asked me if it would be possible to put a prison underground. They probably meant buried, out of sight, but I wouldn't go that far. And since this was pro bono work I could do what I thought best. I sent them a little watercolor and kept this copy for myself. It's a bit on the too-green side but I hope you'll overlook that.

Anyway, the idea comes through. Everything faces inward to a huge central courtyard. From outside, all you see is a wooded hill surrounded by lawns and gardens ...and a big fence.

I show it here as a reminder that underground buildings come in all shapes and sizes, and are always good for you.

132.

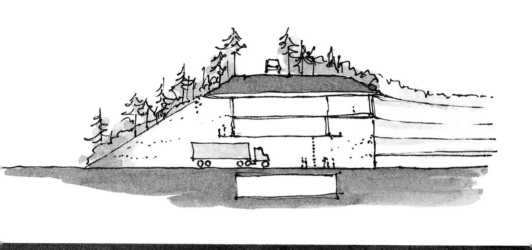

PROTECTIVE EARTH BERM

GARAGE

FLOWER

VE
GA

(NIGHT)

FRUIT TREES

PLANTED PRIVACY MOUND AND NOISE BARRIER

POROUS PAVING PROVIDES GREEN DRIVEWAY AND ALLOWS RAIN TO SOAK INTO SOIL.

PEBBLE
FOR RA

AN ABOVE·GROUND UNDERGROUND HOUSE

GREENHOUSE-TYPE FOYER   NORTH SIDE SHELTER
                        PLANTING AND
      SHED   WILDLIFE AREA

                                    EARTH
                                    BERM

                                    PRIVATE
                                    SOUTH SIDE
                                    SUN COURT

EN GARDEN   SOUTH SIDE GLASS SOLAR WALL
R PERCOLATION   NATIVE TREES, PLANTS, & GROUND COVERS

135.

A hillside research "campus" of offices, labs, and residences for a think-tank relocating from Hong Kong will be built on a site in Indiana. Earth covered, it will also have photovoltaic power, composting toilets, porous paving, and, of course, reforestation with native plants.

The project is moving very slowly but the site has been purchased and I have great hopes for the eventual completion of the work.

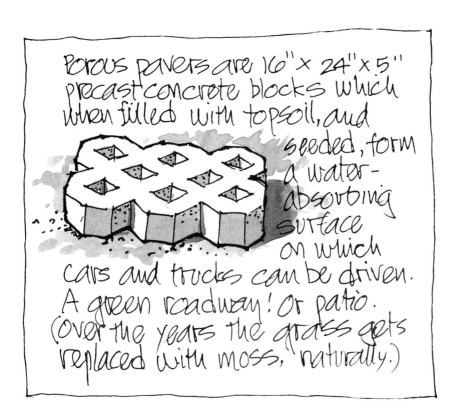

Porous pavers are 16" x 24" x 5" precast concrete blocks which when filled with topsoil, and seeded, form a water-absorbing surface on which cars and trucks can be driven. A green roadway! or patio. (over the years the grass gets replaced with moss, naturally.)

137.

This is the place to say goodbye,
I guess. If you've managed to
hang on this far I salute you
and wish you the best.
I hope you'll far exceed
my best expectations for you.

    Sincerely, MALCOM UEUS

Cape Cod, Massachusetts, 1999.

P.S.

100 years ago it was 1899 – or some other year, depending upon when you're reading this. Back then, if we could have aired pictures of today's familiar world even the most imaginative futurist would have found it hard to believe that so much could have been done in a single century.

Looking back the other way to 1799, that same futurist had seen what, until then, had seemed like profound changes: defeat of all the Indian nations, a great civil war, an end to slavery, a transcontinental railroad, telegraphs, telephones, steamships, and massive immigration – but that first U.S. century could hardly compare to the second. Not only have we the usual examples – planes, cars, T.V., space travel, computers – we have the sheer vastness of everything as well: farms feeding hundreds of millions while farm employment (which once had been number one) stands at less than 5% of all U.S. jobs, cities 50 and 100 miles across, spreading over the green land, horrendous nuclear wastes ticking away with no safe repository in sight, and a consumer society so wasteful our debris

141.

threatens in places to bury us.

If we created the worst of those problems in 100 years we can certainly correct them in another hundred. Seen as one staggeringly huge challenge it may seem impossible to solve but seen as a succession of smaller ones it falls nicely into perspective.

Still, with regard to the killing of land by buildings, not one architect in a hundred today sees underground architecture as the needed alternative. Instead, the profession prefers band-aids and smoke screens like clustered buildings and more parks. The resistance to underground architecture is due not only to inertia and unfamiliarity with earth-type building techniques but to fear of ridicule and fear of failure as well.

Another negative factor is our increasingly distant relationship to nature. We live and work in totally artificial environments. Wild nature, the eternal base condition of the planet, is now unimportant to most of us.

But it doesn't really matter what we architects think. We have become irrelevant. This will soon be a political issue. When the votes are there the ball will start to roll, architects or no architects, and we'll be off and running.

The Story of My Life

I was born in 1926, became an architect in 1953, and began to design underground buildings in 1964. Now, 35 years later, in spite of my having lectured at almost every U.S. architectural school, been on network T.V., and written 15 or 20 books on the subject, underground architecture is still virtually unknown. So much for my effectiveness.

This has disappointed me now and then but I'm sure time is running out for land-killing projects, and I happily await their certain demise.